Zen Mind, Calm Life

A Practical Guide to Mastering Stress Management for Inner Peace

Hu Tien

All rights reserved. No part of this publication may be reproduced, distributed, or transmitted in any form or by any means, including photocopying, recording, or other electronic or mechanical methods, without the prior written permission of the publisher, except in the case of brief quotations embodied in critical reviews and certain other noncommercial uses permitted by copyright law.

Copyright © Hu Tien
(2023)

Contents

- **INTRODUCTION** 4
  - ZEN AND ZEN MIND 8
  - DO I NEED ZEN MIND? 15
  - WHAT IS STRESS 18
  - WHAT IS MANAGEMENT AND STRESS MANAGEMENT 20
- **CHAPTER 1** 22
- **UNVEILING THE POWER OF ZEN** 22
  - The right practice 26
  - Practice 2 30
- **CHAPTER 2** 34
- **BREAKING THE STRESS CYCLE** 34
- **CHAPTER 3** 40
- **MINDFULNESS MEDITATION** 40
  - YOUR GATEWAY TO SERENITY 40
- **CHAPTER 4** 45
- **NAVIGATING CHAOS WITH EQUANIMITY** 45
- **CHAPTER 5** 50
- **SIMPLIFYING YOUR LIFE** 50
  - The Path to Tranquility 50
- **CHAPTER 6** 55
- **MASTERING STRESS IN DAILY LIFE** 55
- **CONCLUSION** 63

INTRODUCTION

My venture into the realm of Zen Mind has been both illuminating and revolutionary. Since the moment I crossed this path, I sensed a profound change in the way I perceive the world. The core of the Zen Mind, marked by its focus on presence and mindfulness, has fundamentally changed how I engage with my environment and my thoughts.

When I initially tried to meditate in the traditional Zen manner, I encountered a notable challenge. My mind, accustomed to its constant internal dialogue, resisted the tranquility I was aiming to foster. However, with perseverance, something remarkable occurred. I began observing my thoughts impartially, allowing them to flow like a river without attachment. This seemingly simple yet potent act of detached observation offered me a glimpse into the inner serenity promised by Zen Mind.

Through consistent meditation, I grasped the art of relinquishing my ties to the past and concerns about the future. I started comprehending the impermanent nature of all things, leading to a sense of liberation. This realization seamlessly integrated into my daily life, enabling me to approach each moment with newfound acceptance and gratitude.

Zen teachings often underscore the significance of complete presence in every endeavor, whether it's washing dishes, strolling, or attentively listening to others. Gradually, I assimilated this mindfulness into my life, revealing the astonishing depth in even the simplest tasks. The flavors of food became more vibrant, the hues around me more vivid, and my interactions with others more authentic.

Arguably, one of the most transformative elements of my experience with Zen Mind has been the dissolution of the boundary between myself and the world. This dissolution isn't a forfeiture of individuality, but rather an expansion of consciousness. I came to realize my integral role in the intricate fabric of existence, intertwined with everything and everyone. This interconnectedness cultivated a sense of compassion and empathy that I hadn't fully known before.

While my journey with Zen Mind is still unfolding, the undeniable changes within me are evident. I've learned that the goal isn't to attain a specific state of mind but to embrace the ongoing journey of self-discovery and inner growth. The teachings of the Zen Mind encompass a delicate dance between effort and surrender, a dance that continues to shape my life in unforeseen ways.

My encounter with Zen Mind has been a transformative voyage into the depths of my consciousness. It's a voyage marked by self-awareness, mindfulness, and interconnectedness, steadily revealing itself with each passing day. This path has presented me with a fresh perspective to perceive the world, and I'm endlessly appreciative of the tranquility and wisdom it has bestowed upon me.

ZEN AND ZEN MIND

Zen is a term that originates from the Japanese pronunciation of the Chinese word "Chán" (禪), which in turn comes from the Sanskrit word "Dhyāna." The term is used to refer to a school of Mahayana Buddhism that emphasizes meditation, mindfulness, and direct experience to achieve enlightenment. While the term "Zen" is most commonly associated with Japanese Zen Buddhism, it also has counterparts in other East Asian languages:

Chinese: Chán (禪)
Korean: Seon (선)
Vietnamese: Thiền

In each of these languages, the term refers to the same school of Buddhism that focuses on the practice of meditation and direct insight to attain enlightenment. While the term is pronounced differently in various languages, the core concepts and practices remain consistent across Zen traditions in different countries.

Therefore **"Zen Mind"** refers to a state of awareness and philosophy connected to Zen Buddhism. It's marked by a profound consciousness of the present moment, mindfulness, and being fully engaged. The term "Zen" is derived from the Chinese word "Chán," which comes from the Sanskrit "Dhyāna," signifying meditation.

The concept of Zen Mind entails a mindset devoid of distractions, biases, and mental clutter. It's about complete involvement in the current activity, whether it's meditation, daily tasks, or work. The purpose of nurturing a Zen Mind is to attain a deep comprehension of reality and existence.

Several elements define the notion of the Zen Mind

Presence: Practicing Zen involves wholeheartedly existing in the present instant, unburdened by the past or the future. This enables unmediated, unfiltered contact with reality.

Mindfulness: Zen promotes heightened consciousness of thoughts, emotions, and surroundings. This mindfulness is impartial and accepting.

Simplicity: Zen often advocates simplicity and minimalism both in the physical environment and mental processes. This aids in minimizing distractions and focusing on what truly holds value.

Non-attachment: Zen Mind entails releasing attachments to material possessions, desires, and even intense emotions. This doesn't imply avoiding these aspects, but rather not allowing them to govern or determine one's identity.

Emptiness: In Zen philosophy, "emptiness" doesn't denote literal nothingness. Instead, it signifies that all things are interrelated and lack an independent, permanent essence. This realization can lead to a sense of liberation and insight.

Direct Experience: Zen prioritizes direct experiential comprehension over solely depending on intellectual concepts. It encourages individuals to personally encounter truth instead of relying solely on teachings.

Koans: These are paradoxical inquiries or statements presented by Zen masters to students, aiding them in breaking free from conventional thinking and reaching deeper insight.

Zazen: This is seated meditation, a fundamental practice in Zen Buddhism. Practitioners focus on their breath and observe thoughts without attachment.

"Zen Mind" encompasses an approach to life with an open and lucid mind, striving to transcend dualities and attain a profound feeling of interconnectedness and enlightenment. It's a voyage of self-discovery and inner serenity that surpasses verbal expression and concepts.

A BRIEF HISTORY OF ZEN

Zen denotes a branch of Mahayana Buddhism originating in China during the Tang dynasty (7th century) and subsequently spreading to other parts of East Asia, including Japan. It centers on firsthand experience and inner understanding of one's essence as a path to achieving enlightenment.

A condensed chronicle of Zen unfolds as follows

Emergence in China (6th to 9th centuries): Zen's inception can be linked back to early Chan Buddhism, brought to China from India by Bodhidharma in the 6th century. Known as Chan in China, this approach prioritized meditation and immediate experience over-dependence on scriptures and rituals. With time, Chan branched into diverse schools, with influential figures such as Huineng and Linji contributing to its progression.

Transmission to Japan (12th century): Zen Buddhism reached Japan in the 12th century and was referred to as "Zen." The Japanese variant drew inspiration from multiple Chinese schools, with Rinzai and Soto being the most prominent. Rinzai emphasized intense meditation (zazen) and the employment of koans (paradoxical statements or queries) to trigger insights. Conversely, the Soto school underscored serene and prolonged meditation, regarding enlightenment as inherent in everyday actions.

Evolution in Japan (13th to 19th centuries): Zen Buddhism emerged as a significant cultural and spiritual influence in Japan, leaving its mark on art, literature, tea ceremonies, martial arts, and more. Zen meditation took root among samurai, artists, and common people alike. Different Zen temples and monasteries were established, each aligned with the teachings of distinct Zen masters.

Contemporary Period and Western Impact (20th **century and beyond**): Zen garnered global attention in the 20th century, partially due to the writings of D.T. Suzuki, a Japanese scholar who introduced Zen philosophy to the Western world. Many Westerners developed an interest in Zen's direct approach to spirituality and meditation. Integration of Zen concepts into Western psychology, philosophy, and popular culture (like the Beat Generation of writers) further elevated its prominence.

Worldwide Influence and Present-Day Practice: At present, Zen Buddhism is practiced internationally, adapting to local cultures and evolving in various expressions. Zen centers, temples, and meditation retreats can be found globally. Zen's emphasis on mindfulness, being present, and direct experience continues to resonate with individuals seeking a contemplative and experiential route to spirituality and self-discovery.

Across its history, Zen has been distinguished by its emphasis on firsthand experience, meditation, and the pursuit of personal insight and enlightenment. Its enduring influence spans Eastern and Western societies, impacting not only religious customs but also art, philosophy, and daily existence.

DO I NEED ZEN MIND?

Yes, in a world characterized by constant noise, distractions, and the demands of modern life, the concept of the Zen mind has gained increasing significance.
Zen Mind, is linked with mindfulness and meditation techniques, which offers a spectrum of advantages that may prove valuable to you:

Mitigation of Stress: Should you be grappling with stress, anxiety, or a sensation of being overwhelmed, Zen Mind practices can aid in fostering serenity and tranquility. Techniques involving mindful meditation can instruct you to observe your thoughts impartially, diminishing the impact of stressors on your well-being.

Augmented Concentration: Zen Mind practices advocate an elevated state of mindfulness and presence. If you frequently find yourself getting distracted or grappling with focus-related difficulties, these practices can bolster your ability to concentrate and sustain attention.

Clarity of Mind: Using Zen Mind practices, you can master the skill of letting go of racing thoughts and nurturing mental lucidity. This, in turn, can lead to more proficient decision-making and adeptness in problem-solving.

Control of Emotions: The mindfulness methods taught within Zen Mind can assist you in becoming more attuned to your emotional states. This enhanced self-awareness can result in improved emotional regulation and a heightened capacity to navigate challenging circumstances.

Elevated Well-Being: A multitude of individuals discover that regular meditation and mindfulness practices foster an overall heightened sense of well-being. You might encounter greater satisfaction, happiness, and an enhanced optimistic perspective on life.

Self-Exploration: Zen Mind practices frequently involve self-reflection and introspection. If you're on a quest to delve into a more profound understanding of yourself or are in search of personal maturation and advancement, these practices can prove advantageous.

Bettered Relationships: Mindfulness practices can lead you to be more present and attentive during your interactions with others. This can pave the way for enriched communication, empathy, and more robust interpersonal connections.

Spiritual Quest: For those treading a spiritual path, Zen Mind can offer a route to forging a connection with a more profound sense of purpose, self-awareness, and interconnectedness.

WHAT IS STRESS

Stress serves as a necessary classroom that everyone must complete.
In other words, stress is the body's physiological and psychological response triggered when an individual perceives a demand or pressure that surpasses their ability to handle it. This reaction is a natural response to a variety of challenges, shifts, or threats in the surroundings. The body's response to stress involves a complex series of hormonal and physiological changes that often result in increased alertness, tension, and cmotional unease.

External factors, such as work deadlines, financial worries, or relationship conflicts, as well as internal factors like personal expectations, fears, and concerns, can all contribute to stress. Although some degree of stress can serve as motivation and aid individuals in facing challenges, prolonged or excessive stress can have adverse impacts on physical health, mental state, and overall quality of life.

Effectively managing stress entails adopting healthy coping strategies, practicing relaxation methods, and seeking assistance when necessary. This is crucial because chronic stress has the potential to contribute to an array of health problems, including anxiety, depression, heart-related issues, and a compromised immune system.

WHAT IS MANAGEMENT AND STRESS MANAGEMENT

Management is The art or expertise of effectively managing individuals or circumstances.

Stress management, therefore, is the effective recognition, addressing, and alleviating of the physical, emotional, and psychological pressures that stem from various life challenges, demands, and circumstances. It encompasses the adoption of strategies, methods, and practices to handle and minimize the adverse impacts of stress on one's overall well-being, health, and quality of life. Stress management encompasses a variety of approaches, including techniques for relaxation, efficient time utilization, problem-solving abilities, emotional control, making health-conscious choices in lifestyle, and seeking assistance from professionals or social networks. The objective of stress management is to cultivate resilience, enhance coping mechanisms, and encourage a healthier response to stressors, ultimately leading to a more well-rounded and harmonious lifestyle.

CHAPTER 1

UNVEILING THE POWER OF ZEN

The rapid and demanding pace of contemporary life frequently results in people feeling overwhelmed, stressed, and disconnected from their inner selves. Many individuals seek ancient wisdom, like the teachings of Zen, to find solace and clarity amid the chaos, in pursuit of inner peace and a serene existence. This chapter will explore the profound influence of Zen philosophy and its role in effectively managing stress to attain inner tranquility.

The Path to Inner Peace through Zen: Releasing Attachments

Central to Zen is the concept of detachment and the release of attachments. In the context of managing stress, this idea holds immense significance. Clinging to worries, desires, and expectations burdens us mentally and emotionally, contributing to stress. Zen guides us to detach from these attachments, enabling us to face challenges with a clear and unburdened mind.

The Practice of Mindfulness Meditation: Anchoring the Present

Mindfulness meditation is a cornerstone of Zen practice. This technique involves consciously and non-judgmentally focusing on the present moment. By anchoring the mind in the "here and now," individuals can break free from the cycle of ruminating on the past or worrying about the future. Regular mindfulness meditation can lead to improved emotional control, decreased anxiety, and heightened inner serenity.

Nurturing Acceptance and Equanimity: Embracing the Present Reality

Zen philosophy teaches us to acknowledge the impermanence of life and find contentment in our current circumstances, no matter how challenging they may be. This practice of equanimity allows us to approach life's ups and downs with a sense of equilibrium, minimizing the impact of stressors on our mental well-being.

Simplicity and Minimalism: Freeing the Mind

In a world saturated with consumerism and materialism, Zen advocates for simplicity and minimalism. By decluttering our physical environment and simplifying our lives, we can create an environment conducive to tranquility and concentration. A clutter-free space often translates to a clutter-free mind, fostering calmness and mental clarity.

Zen's Role in Stress Management: Practical Applications
Incorporating Zen philosophy into daily life necessitates deliberate effort and consistent practice.

This part will examine how one can infuse Zen principles into stress management strategies

Breath Awareness: Focusing on the breath serves as an anchor to the present moment, aiding in calming the mind and reducing stress.

Mindful Work: Introducing mindfulness into work routines enhances concentration, productivity, and overall job satisfaction.
Mindful Eating: Attentiveness to the sensory experience of eating cultivates gratitude and prevents stress-driven overeating.

Nature Connection: Spending time in nature aligns with Zen's reverence for the natural world and provides a tranquil backdrop for introspection.

Embracing Zen for Everlasting Inner Peace

In a world fraught with diversions, obligations, and stressors, the potency of Zen philosophy stands as a source of optimism for those seeking enduring inner peace. By embracing detachment, mindfulness, acceptance, simplicity, and equanimity, individuals can navigate life's trials with lucidity and serenity. Through persistent practice and dedication to self-awareness, mastering stress management through Zen principles becomes a life-altering journey towards a calmer and more enriching existence.

The right practice

Posture: Maintaining an appropriate physical stance during meditation holds significant importance in Zen philosophy. The customary posture entails sitting with legs crossed on a cushion, maintaining a strapline and relaxed shoulders, and positioning hands in a specific gesture known as a mudra. This posture is crucial for staying alert and minimizing distractions.

Breathing:Controlled breathing is a fundamental aspect of Zen practice. It involves focusing on natural, deep breaths and observing each inhalation and exhalation without attempting to manipulate or change them. This heightened awareness of breath serves as an anchor to the present moment, enhancing mindfulness.

Control: Zen teachings advocate for developing mastery over one's thoughts and emotions. Practitioners are encouraged to liberate themselves from being enslaved by passing thoughts or emotional fluctuations. This entails observing thoughts without getting attached or averse to them, allowing them to naturally arise and fade without disturbance.

Mind Waves:Zen likens the activity of the mind to waves on the surface of the water. The objective is to quiet these mental waves through the practice of meditation and mindfulness. During meditation, one observes the movements of the mind, gradually pacifying its incessant chatter.

Mind Weeds:Mind weeds symbolize distractions and unnecessary thoughts that hinder mindfulness. In Zen, individuals strive to identify and eliminate these mental "weeds" by returning their focus to the present moment. This process fosters mental clarity and a heightened sense of concentration.

The Essence of Zen:The "essence" or core teachings of Zen encapsulate the fundamental principles guiding practitioners towards enlightenment. These teachings often revolve around concepts such as impermanence, non-attachment, and direct experiential understanding beyond conceptual thinking.

Non-Dualism: Zeemphasizeson transcending the dualistic nature of opposites, such as good and bad, self and others, or enlightenment and delusion. This principle encourages perceiving the interconnectedness of all things and adopting a holistic perspective.

Bowing:In Zen, bowing signifies a physical expression of humility, respect, and gratitude. It's not an act of worship towards external deities but rather a gesture that acknowledges the inherent Buddha nature within oneself and all beings. Bowing promotes a sense of humility and interconnectedness.

Ordinary Yet Profound:The Zen Teaching of "Nothing Special" highlights the significance of recognizing the extraordinary within the ordinary aspects of life. It prompts individuals to realize the inherent value in each moment, task, and experience. By nurturing mindfulness, practitioners unveil the depth and richness of daily existence.

Zen Practice as a Journey:Engaging in Zen practice constitutes an ongoing voyage of continual learning and self-discovery. Approaching these practices with an open mind, patience, and a willingness to embrace challenges and insights is paramount. By incorporating these principles into daily life, one embarks on a transformative attitude towards attaining greater inner tranquility, clarity, and a harmonious way of being.

Practice 2

Meditation, known as **Zazen**, stands as the cornerstone of Zen practice. Zazen's essence lies in the act of seated meditation, where one simply observes their thoughts without becoming attached to them. Create a calm and comfortable space for sitting.

Assume a cross-legged position, usually on a cushion or mat, or sit on a chair with feet flat on the ground.

Maintain a straight yet relaxed back, allowing the spine to naturally align.

Place your hands on your lap with palms facing upward, one hand resting atop the other, and thumbs gently touching.
Lower your chin and direct your gaze about a meter ahead without focusing on anything specific.

Breathe naturally, directing your attention to your breath or bodily sensations. When thoughts emerge, acknowledge them without judgment and gently shift your focus back to your breath.

Mindfulness in daily life finds emphasis in Zen. This involves being wholly present and engaged in whatever activity you're engaged in—whether it's eating, walking, or even washing dishes. Focus on each action, sensation, and experience without distractions.

Ethical living, or the practice of precepts, forms a significant aspect of Zen. Precepts are ethical guidelines that steer your conduct and interactions with others. They typically encompass refraining from causing harm, being truthful, cultivating generosity, and more.

Guidance from a Zen teacher or participation in a Zen community **(sangha)** proves valuable for many. A teacher offers direction, instruction, and insights that can deepen your practice.

Regular silent retreats, known as sessions, are customary in Zen practice. During these intensive retreats, practitioners engage in extensive meditation and mindfulness, often spanning multiple days.
Sesshin provides a dedicated time for refining practice and insight.

Kinhin, or walking meditation, is often practiced between seated meditation sessions. Walk slowly in a circular or linear path, coordinating your steps with your breath. The intention is to maintain meditative awareness while in motion.

Formal rituals and ceremonies are integrated into Zen to enhance practice and cultivate mindfulness. These rituals may involve bowing, chanting, and other symbolic acts.

Studying Zen texts offers valuable insights and guidance for your practice. Classical Zen texts from various masters provide profound wisdom on meditation, mindfulness, and the fundamental nature of existence

CHAPTER 2

BREAKING THE STRESS CYCLE

It is crucial to acknowledge that stress isn't an unavoidable aspect of existence. By adopting the right mindset and employing effective techniques, we have the potential to disrupt the cycle of stress and pave the path to a serene state of mind and a tranquil life.

H is an array of approaches and insights aimed at mastering the management of stress, ultimately leading to the attainment of inner peace.

Understanding the Cycle of Stress
Before we can dismantle the cycle of stress, it's imperative to comprehend its mechanics. Stress is a natural response designed to help us confront challenges and threats. Yet, in modern times, the stressors we face are often abstract and psychological, triggering the same physical reactions without providing the same resolution. This perpetuates a cycle of stress, leading to chronic stress and its detrimental effects on both mental and physical health.

Mindfulness: A Key to Breaking the Cycle
Mindfulness stands out as a powerful tool in disrupting the cycle of stress. It involves being fully present in the present moment, observing our thoughts and emotions without passing judgment. This practice enables us to create a gap between stimuli and our response, granting us the agency to choose how we react. By nurturing mindfulness, we can interrupt the automatic stress response and substitute it with a more measured and composed reaction.

Fostering Resilience
Resilience, the capacity to bounce back from challenges and setbacks, is a trait worth cultivating. Developing resilience doesn't imply avoiding stress, but rather building the inner strength to confront it directly. This entails reframing negative thoughts, practicing self-compassion, and establishing a robust support network. By enhancing our resilience, we can confront stressors with a more balanced outlook, diminishing their impact on our overall well-being.

Harnessing the Influence of Breath and Meditation
Deep breathing exercises and meditation wield substantial influence in disrupting the cycle of stress. Purposeful, profound breathing triggers the relaxation response, slowing our heart rate and calming our thoughts. Regular meditation enhances our ability to

observe our thoughts without becoming entangled in them. This practice fosters detachment from stressors and fosters a sense of inner tranquility.

Effective Time Management and Boundaries
Stress is frequently exacerbated by poor time management and the absence of boundaries. Learning to prioritize tasks, establish realistic objectives, and allocate time for self-care can notably decrease stress levels. Additionally, establishing healthy boundaries in personal and professional relationships prevents the overwhelming sensation of being pulled in multiple directions.

Physical Well-being as a Pillar of Mental Wellness
The intricate connection between the mind and body is undeniable. Engaging in regular physical activity, maintaining a balanced diet, and ensuring adequate sleep are fundamental for managing stress. Exercise stimulates the release of endorphins, natural stress alleviators, while proper nutrition and sleep provide the body with the resources it requires to effectively cope with stress.

Seeking Expert Support
In some instances, dismantling the cycle of stress necessitates more than self-help techniques. When chronic stress persists and significantly impacts our quality of life, seeking assistance from therapists or

counselors can provide valuable tools and coping mechanisms. They can assist in addressing the root causes of stress and developing a customized plan for its management.

Cultivating a Lifestyle Resilient to Stress
Disrupting the cycle of stress is an ongoing endeavor rather than a one-time occurrence. By integrating mindfulness, resilience, healthful habits, and support systems into our daily lives, we can establish a foundation resistant to stress. This equips us to confront challenges with a composed and centered mindset, fostering inner tranquility even amid chaotic situations.

Disrupting the cycle of stress is an essential step toward attaining a serene mind and a tranquil existence By comprehending the dynamics of stress, nurturing mindfulness, cultivating resilience, integrating relaxation techniques, managing time and boundaries, prioritizing physical well-being, and seeking professional assistance when required, we can master stress management and nurture enduring inner peace. It's essential to remember that the journey toward a stress-free life unfolds gradually, marked by self-discovery and personal growth.

CHAPTER 3

MINDFULNESS MEDITATION

YOUR GATEWAY TO SERENITY

An ancient practice exists that provides comfort amidst the chaos of contemporary existence - mindfulness meditation. Rooted in age-old wisdom, mindfulness meditation has arisen as a potent tool for achieving inner calm and nurturing a composed mindset amidst life's turbulence.

Revealing the Core of Mindfulness Meditation
At the heart of mindfulness meditation lies the act of fully inhabiting the present moment, free from judgment or distraction. This practice involves redirecting one's focus to the sensations of breath, bodily sensations, and immediate surroundings. It encourages observing thoughts and emotions without becoming entangled in them. Through consistent engagement, a heightened awareness of one's experiences develops, facilitating clearer and more composed responses to life's challenges.

Cultivating a Tranquil Mind
The concept of a tranquil mind is often illustrated as one that is receptive, peaceful, and unburdened by unnecessary mental clutter. Mindfulness meditation serves as a conduit for nurturing this state of mind. By refining the ability to concentrate on the present moment, individuals learn to release concerns about the past and anxieties about the future. This mental training paves the way for a more serene and centered way of life.

Benefits of Mindfulness Meditation

Alleviating Stress: Stress is an inherent part of life, yet mindfulness meditation equips individuals with effective tools for managing it. Observing thoughts and emotions with detachment prevents them from escalating into overwhelming stressors.

Emotion Regulation: Mindfulness meditation enhances emotional intelligence. It fine-tunes sensitivity to emotions, empowering individuals to respond to them in a balanced and constructive manner.

Enhanced Focus and Concentration: In a world filled with distractions, mindfulness meditation becomes a platform for honing attention. Practicing focus on the breath or physical sensations sharpens the ability to concentrate on tasks across all aspects of life.

Deepened Self-Awareness: Through mindfulness, a richer understanding of oneself takes shape - encompassing thought patterns, emotional triggers, and habitual reactions. This self-awareness empowers deliberate choices rather than impulsive reactions.

Nurturing Compassion: Mindfulness meditation fosters self-compassion and empathy towards others. The practice of treating oneself with kindness and impartiality naturally extends to those in one's surroundings.

Integration of Mindfulness into Daily Routine
While mindfulness meditation is often associated with seated stillness, its essence can be woven into various facets of daily life. Engaging in mindful eating, relishing each bite, or practicing mindful walking, focusing on each footstep, showcasing its integration. Even ordinary chores like washing dishes can morph into opportunities for mindfulness.

Embarking on the Mindfulness Journey
Beginning a voyage into mindfulness meditation requires no elaborate equipment or specialized training. Starting with brief sessions - even just 5 to 10 minutes each day - and gradually extending them as comfort grows is effective. A plethora of resources, such as guided meditation apps, online videos, and literature, are accessible to support this journey.

In a world that constantly demands our attention and energy, cultivating a serene mindset through mindfulness meditation emerges as a valuable skill. It provides a sanctuary of inner tranquility amidst the commotion, empowering skillful navigation of life's trials with grace and peace. Over time, mindfulness meditation evolves from a mere technique into a lifestyle that nurtures heightened self-awareness, emotional well-being, and a profound connection to the present moment.

CHAPTER 4

NAVIGATING CHAOS WITH EQUANIMITY

Amidst the busy and fast-paced nature of modern life, chaos often accompanies us without fail. The continuous demands stemming from work, relationships, and personal aspirations can lead to an overwhelming feeling that disrupts our inner serenity. However, as we delve into the realm of a Zen mindset and a tranquil existence, we come to realize that it's possible to navigate through life's disorder with a sense of equanimity – a state of mind that's balanced and serene.

Understanding Equanimity
Equanimity is frequently described as the ability to maintain a sense of balance and composure regardless of external circumstances. It's not about displaying indifference or apathy, but rather about cultivating a deep sense of inner stability. This mental state empowers us to

respond to challenges and chaos with clarity and centeredness.

The Essence of Chaos
In this context, chaos refers to the unpredictable and often overwhelming aspects of life that can trigger stress and anxiety. This could encompass unforeseen events, demanding schedules, conflicts in relationships, and more. It's crucial to acknowledge that chaos is a natural element of existence – life inherently possesses dynamism and constant change. Instead of attempting to eliminate chaos, the focus shifts towards nurturing an inner resilience to confront it.

Zen's Perspective on Chaos
Zen philosophy accentuates the impermanence and interconnectivity of all things. According to the Zen viewpoint, chaos is merely another facet of existence, and our aversion to it arises from our attachment to stability and control. By embracing the fundamental nature of impermanence, we can learn to navigate through chaotic situations without losing our equilibrium. Zen teachings encourage us to release rigid expectations and surrender to the flow of life.

Practical Approaches to Cultivate Equanimity

Breath Awareness: The breath serves as an anchor to the present moment. During turbulent times, dedicating a few moments to focus on your breath can aid in regaining composure and gaining a fresh perspective.

Self-Compassion: Treating oneself with kindness and understanding is paramount. When confronted with chaos, self-compassion prevents self-criticism and fosters a nurturing attitude toward one's well-being.

Reducing External Inputs: Temporarily disconnecting from the constant stream of information can offer relief from chaos. Engaging in digital detoxes or quiet retreats can aid in regaining mental clarity.

Embracing Silence: Regularly seeking silence and solitude creates room for introspection and rejuvenation. Amidst the silence, we can more effectively discern what truly matters amidst the chaos.

Incorporating Equanimity into Daily Life
Cultivating equanimity is a continuous journey that necessitates consistent practice. It's about weaving the principles of a Zen mindset into your daily routine, even in moments of disorder. By approaching challenges with a composed and centered demeanor, you can ease the intensity of chaos and confront situations with enhanced wisdom and clarity.

Mastering the art of navigating chaos with equanimity has the potential to reshape how we perceive life's trials. By embracing the fundamental teachings of Zen philosophy and integrating practical strategies, we can construct a tranquil inner landscape that remains undisturbed even amidst chaos. This proficiency in managing stress paves the path toward a life characterized by profound inner peace.

CHAPTER 5

SIMPLIFYING YOUR LIFE

The Path to Tranquility

Simplifying your life involves a process of relinquishing attachments – letting go of belongings, activities, and even relationships that no longer align with your authentic self. This act of releasing should not be seen as a loss; rather, it opens the door to gaining tranquility, mental clarity, and heightened focus. Through decluttering physical spaces, streamlining commitments, and reassessing priorities, you create space for what truly holds value.

Minimalism as a Lifestyle Choice

Minimalism, often seen as an extreme form of simplification, has gained prominence as a lifestyle choice that encourages intentional living and mindful consumption. Embracing minimalism doesn't necessarily mean adopting an austere lifestyle; instead, it prompts you to surround yourself with experiences and possessions that genuinely bring joy and significance. This shift in perspective helps break free from societal pressures of materialism and accumulation, leading to a lighter, more serene existence.

Digital Detox and Unplugging
In our technology-dominated era, digital clutter is as overwhelming as physical clutter. Constant notifications, social media updates, and the compulsion to remain connected around the clock contribute to a restless mind. Regularly practicing digital detoxes and consciously unplugging can provide relief from the digital chaos. By establishing specific spaces and times for online interaction, you regain control over your focus and create moments of stillness and mindfulness.

Mindful Time Management
An overcrowded schedule can be just as stressful as a cluttered physical space. Mindful time management involves adopting a less-is-more approach, prioritizing quality over quantity. By concentrating on essential tasks, setting boundaries, and learning to decline when necessary, you make room for meaningful experiences and revitalize activities that nurture your inner tranquility.

Cultivating Inner Space Through Meditation
Meditation serves as a potent tool for internal simplification. By sitting in stillness and observing thoughts without judgment, you learn to declutter your

mind. Regular meditation not only alleviates stress and anxiety but also enhances your capacity for deliberate decision-making and staying present in each moment.

Creating a Sanctuary of Serenity
Crafting living spaces with simplicity and intention can significantly impact your overall sense of peace. Integrating natural elements, utilizing neutral colors, and minimizing decorative items foster tranquility. An organized, clutter-free environment promotes mental clarity and offers a tangible representation of the Zen mind you aim to attain.

Embracing the Journey of Simplification
Simplifying your life is an ongoing process rather than a final destination. It requires a commitment to continuous self-awareness, a willingness to reevaluate and adapt, and a steadfast dedication to your well-being. As you gradually release what no longer serves a purpose and create room for joy, you pave the way for a life characterized by equilibrium, harmony, and lasting inner peace.

In essence, simplifying your life is a conscious decision to disentangle yourself from the complexities of modern living. By embracing minimalism, practicing mindful time management, and cultivating inner serenity, you embark on a transformative expedition toward achieving a Zen mind and a peaceful life. This chapter has highlighted the importance of simplification as a route to tranquility, equipping you with the means to declutter both your external and internal worlds, ultimately guiding you toward a life marked by serenity and harmony

CHAPTER 6

MASTERING STRESS IN DAILY LIFE

Amidst the rapid pace and commotion of modern life, stress has become an unwelcome companion for many. The unceasing demands of work, personal obligations, and societal pressures can leave us feeling inundated and tense. However, the wisdom of Zen philosophy offers valuable insights and practices that can assist us in conquering stress and nurturing inner serenity sinn serenity in f chaos.

Grasping the Essence of Stress
Before embarking on the quest to master stress, it is imperative to comprehend its essence. Stress frequently emerges from our perceptions and reactions to external situations. Zen philosophy guides us to embrace the concept of impermanence – the realization that everything is transient. By acknowledging the fleeting nature of circumstances, we liberate ourselves from unnecessary attachments and diminish the control stress exertions.

The Influence of Breath
Breath stands as a foundational element of Zen meditation. It acts as a conduit between the mind and body, providing a tangible focal point. When stress surfaces, deliberately taking deep breaths can aid in centering and calming us. By regulating our breathing, we prompt the body to trigger its relaxation response, thereby reducing the production of stress-inducing hormones. This simple practice connects us with our physical selves and the present instant, serving as a potent tool for managing stress.

Non-Attachment and Release

Zen philosophy advocates for non-attachment – the practice of refraining from excessive attachment to outcomes or possessions. By relinquishing the compulsion to control every facet of our lives, we liberate ourselves from the weight of expectations. This does not entail forsaking responsibility; rather, it involves adopting a flexible mindset that enables us to navigate challenges without succumbing to excessive stress.

Embracing Tranquility and Silence
In a world inundated with noise and perpetual activity, carving out moments of silence and stillness is imperative for stress management. Zen meditation underscores the value of sitting in silence and observing our thoughts as they ebb and flow. This practice augments our self-awareness and aids us in nurturing a sense of inner tranquility that can extend into our daily routines.

Embracing Simplicity
Zen living advocates for simplicity. Often, stress emanates from the clutter – both physical and mental – that accumulates in our lives. By streamlining our physical spaces and simplifying our schedules, we create space for tranquility to flourish. By prioritizing what truly matters and eliminating unnecessary elements, stress loses its grip on us.

Compassion for Ourselves and Others
In the pursuit of mastering stress, it is vital to treat ourselves with kindness and compassion. Zen philosophy underscores the importance of compassion for ourselves and others. When stress emerges, we can counter its effects by treating ourselves gently, recognizing our limitations, and extending understanding to those around us. This fosters a sense of interconnectedness that can counteract the isolating impact of stress. Furthermore, take time each day to express gratitude for the blessings in your life. This simple practice shifts your focus away from stressors and towards the positive aspects of your existence.

Mindful Respiration
Begin your journey toward inner tranquility with the practice of mindful respiration. Find a comfortable seated position, close your eyes, and bring your attention to your breath. Inhale slowly and deeply, noticing the air entering your nostrils, filling your lungs, and then exhaling gradually. Stay fully present with each breath, gently guiding your mind back whenever it starts to wander. This technique not only calms the mind but also anchors you in the present moment.

Simplify Your Environment

The chaos and clutter in your physical surroundings can contribute to mental clutter. Embrace the principles of minimalism by decluttering your living space. Keep only what truly adds value and meaning to your life. An organized and tidy environment can surprisingly have a soothing effect on your mind.

Attentive Nourishment
In our fast-paced lives, we often eat hurriedly, barely paying attention to our meals. Practice mindful eating by savoring every bite. Observe the textures, flavors, and aromas of your food. Eat slowly and purposefully, without distractions. This practice not only deepens your connection to nourishment but also brings you fully into the present moment.

Meditation
Regular meditation is a cornerstone of Zen practice. Find a quiet space, sit in a comfortable position, and close your eyes. Direct your focus to your breath, a mantra, or the sensations in your body. When thoughts arise, acknowledge them without judgment and gently bring your attention back to your chosen point of focus. Over time, meditation helps cultivate a clear and focused mind.

Walking Meditation The Zen practice extends beyond seated meditation. Engage in walking meditation by taking slow, deliberate steps. Focus on the sensation of your feet touching the ground, the movement of your body, and your breath. This practice can be particularly beneficial for those who find extended seated meditation challenging.

Complete Presence in Daily Activities
Zen encourages us to infuse mindfulness into our everyday tasks. Whether it's washing dishes, walking, or brushing your teeth, engage fully in the activity. Avoid multitasking and immerse yourself entirely in the present task. This fosters mindfulness in all aspects of your life.

Embrace Impermanence
A core tenet of Zen involves embracing the reality of change. Recognize that everything is transient, and attachment to possessions, emotions, or circumstances leads to suffering. By embracing the concept of impermanence, you free yourself from unnecessary stress and cultivate a deeper sense of serenity.

As you incorporate these practical steps into your life, you'll gradually discover the transformative power of a Zen mind. Through mindful breathing, meditation, simplicity, and engagement with the present moment, you'll forge a path to lasting inner calm and greater peace in your daily existence.

CONCLUSION

In a society characterized by ceaseless activity and unrelenting demands, the quest for inner tranquility and a serene existence has grown more imperative than ever before. The endeavor to master stress management and attain a Zen-like mindset is not a mere luxury but an essential requirement for preserving our holistic wellness. Throughout our exploration of Zen philosophy and strategies for handling stress, we have come to realize that achieving a peaceful life demands a persistent and mindful undertaking.

As we've explored extensively into the realms of mindfulness, meditation, and the wisdom imparted by Zen masters, it has become evident that the ability to manage stress and foster a calm state of being resides within our consciousness. By embracing the fundamental tenets of mindfulness, we learn to be fully present in each instance, allowing us to detach from concerns about the past and future. This practice teaches us that we ultimately possess agency over our reactions, rather than being passive victims of our circumstances.

Meditation, another cornerstone of Zen philosophy, equips us with the means to explore the depths of our awareness and cultivate a profound sensitivity to our thoughts and emotions. Through regular meditation practice, we can establish a mental haven that remains impervious to external pressures. This inner sanctuary becomes a retreat where we can seek comfort and clarity even amid tumultuous situations.

The teachings of Zen masters guide us to a profound realization – that simplicity and acceptance are pivotal to a tranquil existence. By relinquishing needless attachments and expectations, we liberate ourselves from the weight of excessive desires and self-imposed stress. Zen philosophy encourages us to embrace life as it unfolds, recognizing both its beauty and imperfections. Through this embrace, we find serenity not through avoidance of our challenges, but by transforming our relationship with them.

Integrating these insights into our daily lives necessitates unwavering practice and commitment. It's crucial to bear in mind that the journey toward a Zen-like mindset and a peaceful life is not linear; setbacks and trials will inevitably surface. Nevertheless, these moments of adversity present opportunities for personal development. With each encounter with stress, we can return to the wisdom we've gained, utilizing mindfulness, meditation, and the teachings of Zen to navigate challenges with grace and resilience.

Concluding our exploration of mastering stress management for inner peace underscores that pursuing a Zen mindset is not a finite destination, but an ongoing voyage. It intertwines with the natural rhythms of existence. By nurturing our emotional and mental well-being, we not only enhance our encounters but also radiate positivity and tranquility to the world around us.

In a culture that often exalts busyness and accomplishments, making the conscious choice to prioritize a serene existence grounded in Zen principles is a revolutionary act of self-preservation. It signifies a commitment to our joy and welfare, a recognition that the state of our minds profoundly molds the essence of our lives. The journey to attain a Zen mindset and a tranquil life may present challenges, yet the rewards are immeasurable – a life imbued with lucidity, contentment, and a profound sense of inner serenity.

Made in the USA
Coppell, TX
15 July 2024

34657860R00036